MAIASAURA

and Other Dinosaurs of the Midwest

by Dougal Dixon

illustrated by
Steve Weston and **James Field**

PICTURE WINDOW BOOKS
Minneapolis, Minnesota

Picture Window Books
5115 Excelsior Boulevard
Suite 232
Minneapolis, MN 55416
877-845-8392
www.picturewindowbooks.com

Printed in the United States of America.

Library of Congress Cataloging-in-Publication Data
Dixon, Dougal.
Maiasaura and other dinosaurs of the Midwest /
by Dougal Dixon ; illustrated by Steve Weston &
James Field.
p. cm. — (Dinosaur find)
Includes bibliographical references and index.
ISBN-13: 978-1-4048-2749-3 (hardcover)
ISBN-10: 1-4048-2749-8 (hardcover)
1. Maiasaura—Juvenile literature. 2. Dinosaurs—
United States—Middle West Region—Juvenile
literature. I. Weston, Steve, ill. II. Field, James, 1959– ill.
III. Title. IV. Series: Dixon, Dougal. Dinosaur find.
QE862.O65D589 2007
567.90978—dc22   2006012134

Acknowledgments
This book was produced for Picture Window Books by
Bender Richardson White, U.K.

Illustrations by James Field (cover and pages 4–5, 7,
9, 13, 15) and Steve Weston (pages 11, 17, 19, 21).
Diagrams by Stefan Chabluk.

Photographs copyright Eyewire Inc. pages 12, 16, 20;
iStockphoto pages 6 (Ramsey Houck), 10 (Vera
Bogaerts), 14 (Eric Gauger), 18; Frank Lane Photo
Agency page 8 (Ron Austing).

Consultant: John Stidworthy, Scientific Fellow of
the Zoological Society, London, and former
Lecturer in the Education Department, Natural
History Museum, London.

Reading Adviser: Susan Kesselring, M.A., Literacy
Educator, Rosemount–Apple Valley–Eagan
(Minnesota) School District

Types of dinosaurs
In this book, a red shape at the
top of a left-hand page shows
the animal was a meat-eater.
A green shape shows it was
a plant-eater.

Just how big—or small—
were they?
Dinosaurs were many different
sizes. We have compared their
sizes to one of the following:

Chicken
2 feet (60 centimeters) tall
6 pounds (2.7 kilograms)

Adult person
6 feet (1.8 meters) tall
170 pounds (76.5 kg)

Elephant
10 feet (3 m) tall
12,000 pounds
(5,400 kg)

TABLE OF CONTENTS

Life in the Midwest 4

Maiasaura. 6

Troodon 8

Triceratops. 10

Tyrannosaurus. 12

Ankylosaurus. 14

Parksosaurus. 16

Stygimoloch 18

Leptoceratops. 20

Where Did They Go?. . 22

Glossary 23

To Learn More 24

Index 24

WHAT'S INSIDE?

Dinosaurs! These dinosaurs lived in what is now the midwestern part of North America. Find out how they survived millions of years ago and what they have in common with today's animals.

LIFE IN THE MIDWEST

Dinosaurs lived between 230 million and 65 million years ago. The world did not look the same then. In most parts of the world, the land and seas were not in the same places as today. At the end of the Age of Dinosaurs, the Midwest was an area of forested plains by the side of a shallow sea.

Plant-eating duckbills such as *Maiasaura*, and armored dinosaurs such as *Ankylosaurus*, watched out for meat-eaters, among them *Tyrannosaurus* and *Troodon*.

MAIASAURA

Maiasaura was one of the duck-billed dinosaurs. It nested in herds close to lakes. The herds looked after the young. As soon as the young were strong enough, each *Maiasaura* family moved away to new feeding grounds.

Nesting grounds today

Flocks of flamingos make their nests together at lakesides, just as herds of *Maiasaura* did in the Age of Dinosaurs.

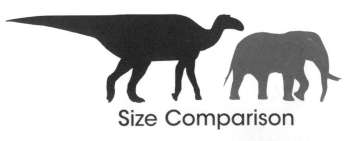

Size Comparison

Maiasaura fed, rested, traveled, and nested together. Their bills had lots of small teeth for grinding plants.

TROODON

Pronunciation:
TROH-o-don

Like *Maiasaura, Troodon* nested in groups by a lakeside. It was a meat-eater, with pointed jaws with lots of sharp little teeth. Parents brought dead dinosaurs back to the nests to feed their babies.

Feeding young today

Hawks and other birds of prey kill small animals, tear them to pieces, and feed the pieces to their young, like *Troodon* did.

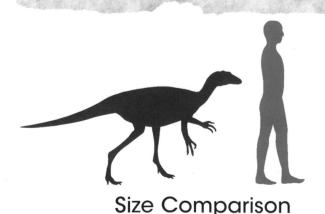

Size Comparison

Troodon chased and killed medium-sized dinosaurs that lived in lakeside forests.

TRICERATOPS

Pronunciation:
tri-SAIR-uh-tops

Triceratops was the biggest of the horned dinosaurs. It had three horns on its armored face and a heavy shield around its neck. It protected itself by turning its head toward an attacker and using its horns as weapons.

Horns today

The bison is a horned animal that travels in herds, just like *Triceratops* did at the end of the Age of Dinosaurs.

Size Comparison

Triceratops lived in big herds. It roamed the plains of the Midwest, looking for new feeding grounds. As well as the horns on its head, there were little horns around the neck frill.

TYRANNOSAURUS

Pronunciation:
tie-RAN-o-SAW-rus

Tyrannosaurus was the biggest meat-eater that ever lived in North America. Its jaws and teeth were huge. It was able to attack the biggest plant-eaters of the time.

Big meat-eaters today

The biggest meat-eating animal in North America today is the grizzly bear. It is big, but not nearly as big as *Tyrannosaurus* was.

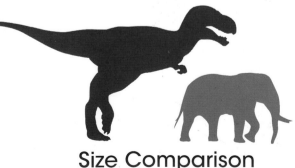

Size Comparison

All of the animals of North America at the end of the Age of Dinosaurs were hunted by *Tyrannosaurus*. They tried to stay clear of those enormous jaws.

13

ANKYLOSAURUS

Pronunciation:
AN-kee-lo-SAW-rus

Ankylosaurus was a big armored dinosaur. It was like a walking tank. Its head, neck, and back were covered in plates, and it had a club on the end of its tail. It ate leaves and plant stems in the forests of the Midwest.

Spiky animals today

The spiny lizard is quite harmless. Like *Ankylosaurus,* it is covered in thick scales and spines to protect itself.

Size Comparison

14

Ankylosaurus munched on low-growing plants. If threatened, the dinosaur would swing its tail against the legs of the attacker.

PARKSOSAURUS

Pronunciation:
PAHRK-suh-SAW-rus

Parksosaurus was a plant-eating dinosaur that lived in the forests. It used its narrow beak to pluck leaves and plant stems to eat. *Parksosaurus* stored the food in its cheeks while it chewed.

Quick escape today

Wild horses run away on their strong legs when they are startled, just like *Parksosaurus* did.

Size Comparison

Parksosaurus was a fairly small, timid dinosaur. It was always on the lookout for meat-eaters that might attack it.

STYGIMOLOCH

What a scary-looking dinosaur *Stygimoloch* was! It had a bony lump on its head that was surrounded by horns and spines. Despite that, *Stygimoloch* was a gentle plant-eating dinosaur.

Spikes today

The horned lizard has a head covered in spines, much like *Stygimoloch* had.

Size Comparison

In addition to its weapons, *Stygimoloch* may have had warning-color patterns on its skin.

LEPTOCERATOPS

Pronunciation:
LEP-tuh-SER-uh-tops

Not all of the horned dinosaurs were huge. *Leptoceratops* was about the size of a sheep. Like its big relatives, *Leptoceratops* fed on leaves that it nipped off trees with its big beak. It had a strong shield around its neck.

Big and small today

Today's tortoises come in all sizes, from as small as your hand to as big as a table. Horned dinosaurs came in different sizes, too.

Size Comparison

Leptoceratops lived in the same place and at the same time as the biggest of the horned dinosaurs, *Triceratops*.

WHERE DID THEY GO?

Dinosaurs are extinct, which means that none of them are alive today. Scientists study rocks and fossils to find clues about what happened to dinosaurs.

People have different explanations about what happened. Some people think a huge asteroid hit Earth and caused all sorts of climate changes, which caused the dinosaurs to die. Others think volcanic eruptions caused the climate to change and that killed the dinosaurs. No one knows for sure what happened to all of the dinosaurs.

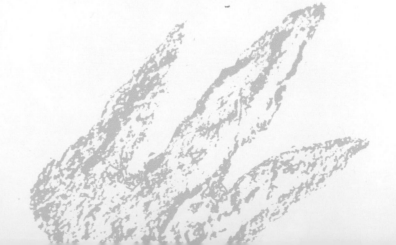

Glossary

armor—protective covering of plates, horns, spikes, or clubs used for fighting

beak—the hard front part of the mouth of birds and some dinosaurs; also called a bill

duckbill—a dinosaur with a broad mouth like a duck's bill that contains hundreds of little teeth for grinding plants

herds—large groups of animals that move, feed, and sleep together

horns—pointed structures on the head, made of bone

jaws—the bones of the face from which teeth grow

plains—large areas of flat land with few large plants

signaling—making a sign, warning, or hint

To Learn More

At the Library

Clark, Neil, and William Lindsay. *1001 Facts About Dinosaurs.* New York: Backpack Books, Dorling Kindersley, 2002.

Gray, Susan H. *Maiasaura.* Chanhassen, Minn.: Child's World, 2004.

Schomp, Virginia. *Maiasaura.* New York: Benchmark Books, 2004.

On the Web

FactHound offers a safe, fun way to find Internet sites related to this book. All of the sites on FactHound have been researched by our staff.

1. Visit *www.facthound.com*
2. Type in this special code for age-appropriate sites: 1404827498
3. Click on the FETCH IT button.

Your trusty FactHound will fetch the best sites for you!

Index

Ankylosaurus, 5, 14–15
armored, 5, 10, 14
babies and young, 6, 8
beak, 16, 20
duck-billed dinosaurs, 5, 6, 7
forests, 4, 9, 14, 16
herds, 6, 11

horned, 10, 18, 20
lakes, 6, 8, 9
Leptoceratops, 20–21
Maiasaura, 5, 6–7, 8
nests, 6, 7, 8
Parksosaurus, 16–17
Stygimoloch, 18–19

tail, 14, 15
teeth, 7, 8, 12
Triceratops, 10–11, 21
Troodon, 5, 8–9
Tyrannosaurus, 5, 12–13

Look for all of the books in the Dinosaur Find series:

Aletopelta and Other Dinosaurs of the West Coast 1-4048-2744-7
Allosaurus and Other Dinosaurs of the Rockies 1-4048-2748-X
Ankylosaurus and Other Mountain Dinosaurs 1-4048-0670-9
Centrosaurus and Other Dinosaurs of Cold Places 1-4048-0672-5
Ceratosaurus and Other Fierce Dinosaurs 1-4048-1327-6
Coelophysis and Other Dinosaurs of the South 1-4048-2747-1
Deltadromeus and Other Shoreline Dinosaurs 1-4048-0669-5
Dromaeosaurus and Other Dinosaurs of the North 1-4048-2745-5
Giganotosaurus and Other Big Dinosaurs 1-4048-1325-X

Maiasaura and Other Dinosaurs of the Midwest 1-4048-2749-8
Nodosaurus and Other Dinosaurs of the East Coast 1-4048-2746-3
Ornithomimus and Other Fast Dinosaurs 1-4048-1326-8
Plateosaurus and Other Desert Dinosaurs 1-4048-0667-9
Saltopus and Other First Dinosaurs 1-4048-1328-4
Scutellosaurus and Other Small Dinosaurs 1-4048-1330-6
Stegosaurus and Other Plains Dinosaurs 1-4048-0668-7
Styracosaurus and Other Last Dinosaurs 1-4048-1329-2
Triceratops and Other Forest Dinosaurs 1-4048-0671-7